I Believe In Santa Claus

I Believe In Santa Claus

Written by

Diane G. Adamson

Illustrated by

M. Chad Randall

To all those who love Santa Claus.
And to my family, friends, teachers,
and mentors, for teaching me that

love is the motivator to goodness.

DGA

Published by North Star Publications
10199 S.W. 201 Terrace, Miami, Florida 33189

ISBN: 0-9673571-0-1

© 1998 Diane Adamson.
Designed by Scott Eggers and Richard Erickson

Reprinted in Korea

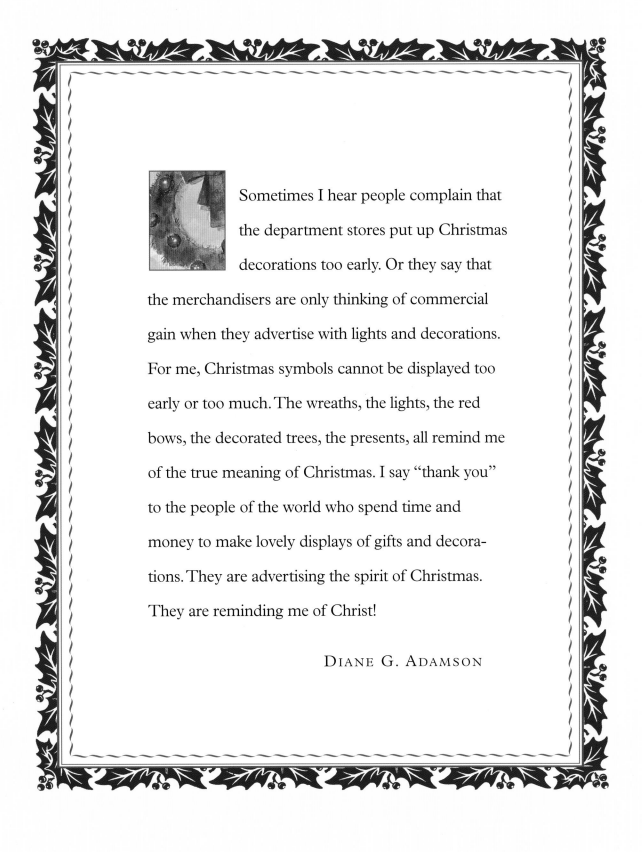 Sometimes I hear people complain that the department stores put up Christmas decorations too early. Or they say that the merchandisers are only thinking of commercial gain when they advertise with lights and decorations. For me, Christmas symbols cannot be displayed too early or too much. The wreaths, the lights, the red bows, the decorated trees, the presents, all remind me of the true meaning of Christmas. I say "thank you" to the people of the world who spend time and money to make lovely displays of gifts and decorations. They are advertising the spirit of Christmas. They are reminding me of Christ!

DIANE G. ADAMSON

I believe in Santa Claus.

Imagine
Santa.

What is he like?

He wears red.

His hair
is white.

He comes in the night.

He loves little children.

He wants us to be good.

And he
brings gifts.

Now imagine Jesus.

What is
He
like?

He wears red.

His hair
is white.

He comes in
the night.

He loves little children.

He *knows*
we are good.

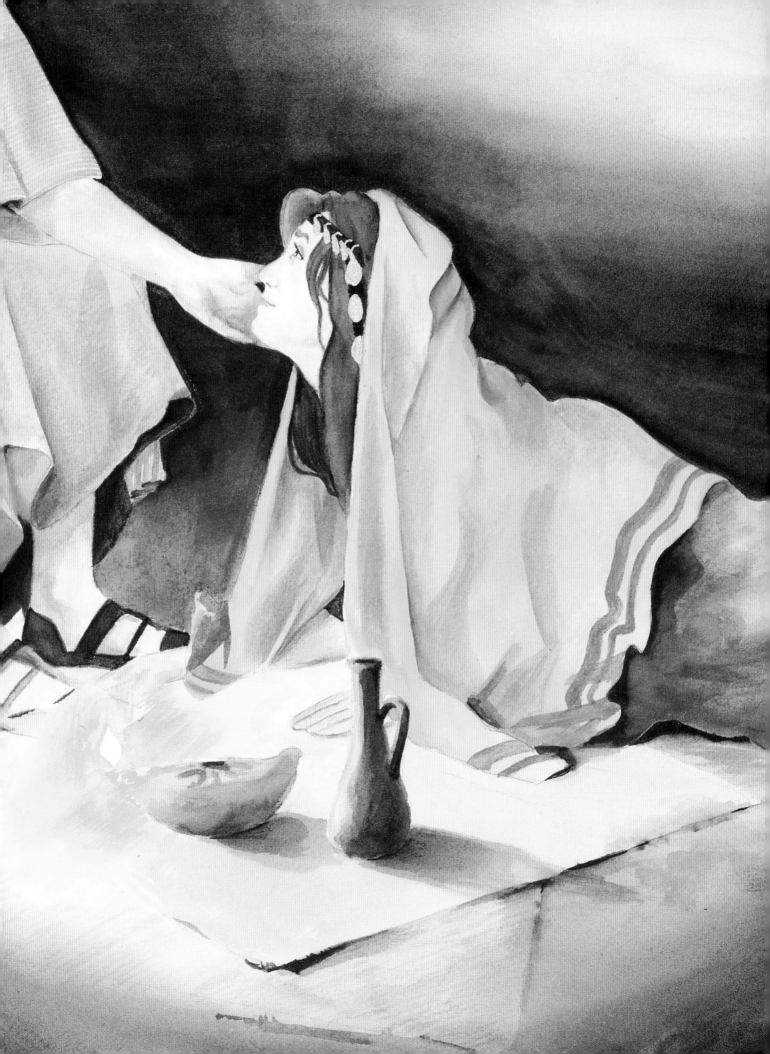

And He
brings gifts.

Santa Claus
is a symbol of
Christmas.

The symbols
of Christmas
can remind us of
the true meaning
of Christmas.

The symbols of Christmas remind me of Christ.

Randall '96

So, I believe in
Santa Claus.

SCRIPTURES

HE WEARS RED.

*Wherefore art thou red in thine apparel, and thy
garments like him that treadeth in the winevat? (Isaiah 63:2)*

HIS HAIR IS WHITE.

*His head and his hairs were white like wool,
as white as snow. (Revelation 1:14)*

HE COMES IN THE NIGHT.

*For yourselves know perfectly that the day of the Lord so
cometh as a thief in the night. (1 Thessalonians 5:2)*

HE LOVES LITTLE CHILDREN.

*But Jesus said, Suffer little children, and forbid
them not, to come unto me: for of such is
the kingdom of heaven. (Matthew 19:14)*

HE *KNOWS* WE ARE GOOD.

*For this is good and acceptable in the sight of our Savior;
Who will have all men to be saved, and to come
unto the knowledge of the truth. (1 Timothy 2:3,4)*

AND HE BRINGS GIFTS.

*Every good gift and every perfect gift is
from above. (James 1:17)*

Symbols

WREATH
Eternal love, no beginning, no end. Love comes full circle.

CANDLE
The light of Christ, our own inner light.

GIFTS
Giving, sharing, thinking of others.

BOW
Tied in the bonds of brotherly love.

BELL
Rings to bring lost sheep home.

TREE
The evergreen of everlasting life, pointing heavenward.

CANDY CANE
Shepherd's crook for bringing lambs back to the fold.

RED
The Savior's sacrifice for all.

STAR
The Bethlehem star, a sign of prophecy, the light of the world.

SANTA CLAUS
The spirit of Christmas, giving and receiving love,
caring, sharing, kindness, cheerfulness, happiness, peace,
good will to all, Christlike living.

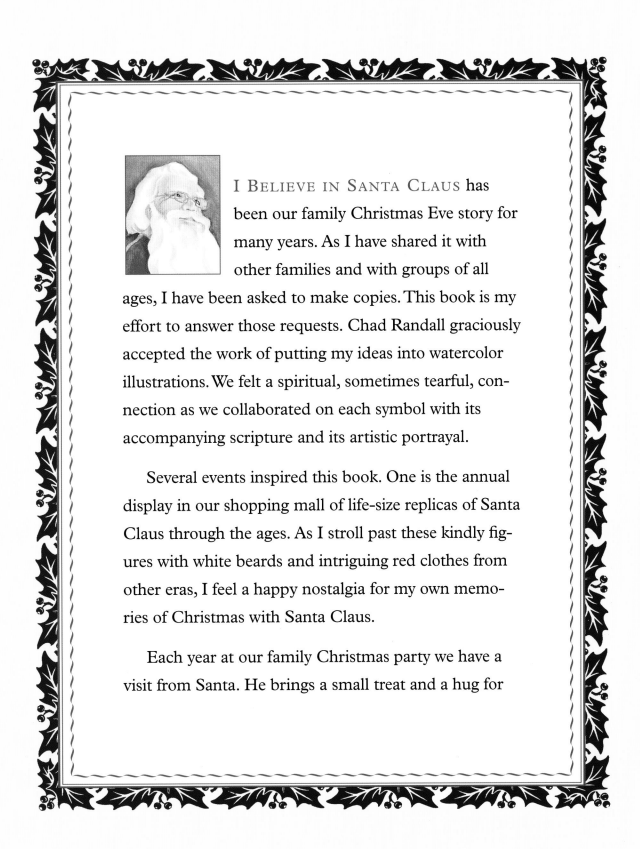

I BELIEVE IN SANTA CLAUS has been our family Christmas Eve story for many years. As I have shared it with other families and with groups of all ages, I have been asked to make copies. This book is my effort to answer those requests. Chad Randall graciously accepted the work of putting my ideas into watercolor illustrations. We felt a spiritual, sometimes tearful, connection as we collaborated on each symbol with its accompanying scripture and its artistic portrayal.

Several events inspired this book. One is the annual display in our shopping mall of life-size replicas of Santa Claus through the ages. As I stroll past these kindly figures with white beards and intriguing red clothes from other eras, I feel a happy nostalgia for my own memories of Christmas with Santa Claus.

Each year at our family Christmas party we have a visit from Santa. He brings a small treat and a hug for each family member and I have noticed that the party becomes more lively and happy after Santa's visit.

Psychologists have written of the healthful benefits of encouraging children to believe in a kind and generous Santa. Strong beliefs in Santa Claus in the tender years are said to foster traits of goodness, helpfulness, and the desire to bring joy and happiness to others. These are all attributes of the Savior and espousing these traits in our own lives not only contributes to healthful living but also helps us to become more Christlike. Parents are counseled to connect the modern Santa Claus with the Christlike St. Nicholas who secretly gave gifts to the poor. By keeping the notion of Santa alive in their family traditions, parents help children learn the spirit of giving to others.

During the Christmas season the spirit of Christ is evident in the cheerful way people greet each other, in the generous donations to the less fortunate, in the many hours of service given, and by the increased shopping as we select gifts for others. There is a spirit of giving and sharing in the very air that comes with no other holiday. Santa Claus represents giving and loving and kind thoughtfulness of others.

All human beings have a basic need to love and be loved. Fantasy is a helpful way for children to feel loved and comforted. Believing in Santa Claus brings happy feelings of love. Children are able to transfer these feelings to the Savior who loves them more than anyone. "We love Him because He first loved us." (1 JOHN 4:19)

When I see the light in my grandchildren's eyes at Christmas time, when I hear stories of past Christmases fondly remembered by my children, and when I see family and friends doing acts of kindness without being found out, then I am very thankful that *I Believe in Santa Claus.*

DIANE GARDNER ADAMSON

$15.95   U.S.A.

ISBN 0-9673571-0-1